A Day in the Life: Grassland Animals

Kori Bustard

Louise Spilsbury

Heinemann
LIBRARY

Chicago, Illinois

www.heinemannraintree.com
Visit our website to find out
more information about
Heinemann-Raintree books.

To order:
☎ Phone 888-454-2279
🖥 Visit www.heinemannraintree.com
to browse our catalog and order online.

Edited by Dan Nunn, Rebecca Rissman, Catherine Veitch,
    and Nancy Dickmann
Designed by Philippa Jenkins
Picture research by Mica Brancic
Originated by Capstone Global Library
Printed and bound in China by South China Printing
    Company Ltd

14 13 12 11 10
10 9 8 7 6 5 4 3 2 1

Library of Congress Cataloging-in-Publication Data
Spilsbury, Louise.
  Kori bustard / Louise Spilsbury.
    p. cm. — (A day in the life. Grassland animals)
  Includes bibliographical references and index.
  ISBN 978-1-4329-4733-0 (hc) — ISBN 978-1-4329-4743-9
(pb) 1. Kori bustard—Juvenile literature. I. Title.
QL696.G86S65 2011
598.3'2—dc22   2010017850

Acknowledgments
We would like to thank the following for permission to
reproduce photographs: Alamy pp. 7, 23 male (© Papilio),
17, 23 female (© AfriPics.com), 20 (© Rick Edwards ARPS),
21 (© Tim Graham); Flickr p. 16 (David Bygott); FLPA p.
12 (Malcolm Schuyl); iStockphoto pp. 4 (© Chris Wiggins),
10 (© Mike Liu), 15 (© brytta), 18, 23 jackal (© Nico Smit);
Photolibrary pp. 13 (age fotostock/Nigel Dennis), 14 (Oxford
Scientific (OSF)), 19 (Oxford Scientific (OSF)/Adrian Bailey);
Photoshot p. 11 (© NHPA/Martin Harvey); Shutterstock pp.
5 (© Riaan van den Berg), 6, 23 crest (© Paul McKinnon), 9,
23 grassland (© Steffen Foerster Photography), 22 (© Braam
Collins), 23 hyena (© Antonio Jorge Nunes), 23 insect (kd2).

Cover photograph of a close-up portrait of a kori bustard in
Etosha National Park, Namibia, reproduced with permission
of Shutterstock (© Johan Swanepoel). Back cover photographs
of (left) the crest of a kori bustard reproduced with permission
of Shutterstock (© Paul McKinnon) and (right) a kori bustard's
nest reproduced with permission of Photolibrary (Oxford
Scientific).

We would like to thank Michael Bright for his invaluable help
in the preparation of this book.

The author would like to dedicate this book to her nephew and
niece, Ben and Amelie: "I wrote these books for animal lovers
like you. I hope you enjoy them". Aunty Louise.

Contents

Some words are in bold, **like this**. You can find out what they mean by looking in the glossary.

What Is a Kori Bustard?

neck

A kori bustard is a big bird that has a long neck.

Kori bustards live alone or in small groups.

Kori bustards can fly, but they do not fly much because they are so heavy.

They spend most days and nights on the ground.

What Do Kori Bustards Look Like?

crest

A kori bustard has a gray neck, and black and white shoulders.

It has a black **crest** and a white stripe over each eye.

An adult **male** kori bustard weighs about the same as a four-year-old boy!

A **female** is much smaller than a male.

Where Do Kori Bustards Live?

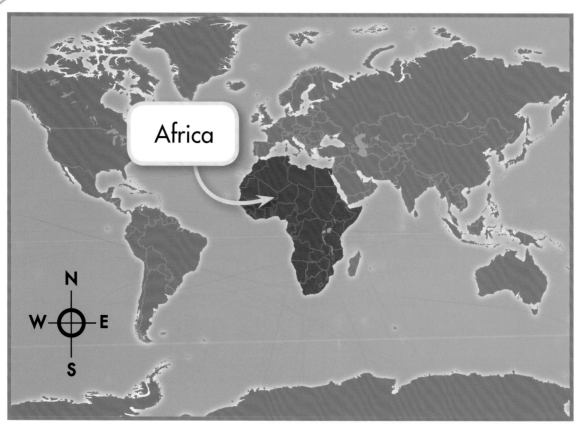

Africa

key: ■ = where kori bustards live

Kori bustards live in parts of southern and eastern Africa.

They mostly live in places called **grasslands**.

In these grasslands the land is covered in grasses and a few trees.

Most days it is hot and dry, but in some months it rains a lot.

What Do Kori Bustards Do During the Day?

Kori bustards look for food in the mornings and afternoons.

At midday when it gets very hot, they rest in a shady spot.

Kori bustards often feed near zebras.

When zebras walk they bring out small animals that kori bustards like to eat.

What Do Kori Bustards Eat?

snake

Kori bustards eat insects and small animals, like mice and snakes.

Sometimes they eat seeds and berries too.

Kori bustards get water from the food they eat.

They also drink from pools of water that fill up during the rainy months.

Where Do Kori Bustards Lay Eggs?

nest

Female kori bustards scrape a shallow pit between grasses for a nest.

This keeps the eggs cool and hidden during the day.

Mothers stay with the eggs day and night.

They throw grass onto their backs so other animals cannot see them.

What Are Kori Bustard Chicks Like?

Chicks are striped so they are hard to see among grasses in the day.

They eat **insects** that their mothers catch for them.

During the day, a chick often walks in its mother's shadow.

This keeps it out of the heat.

Which Animals Hunt Kori Bustards?

jackal

Big animals like **jackals**, eagles, **hyenas**, and lions hunt kori bustards.

When kori bustards are scared, they bark or growl.

Sometimes small birds sit on a kori bustard's back eating **insects**.

They warn kori bustards when danger is near because they suddenly fly off!

What Do Kori Bustards Do at Night?

In the evening, kori bustards find a safe place in long grass.

They use their beak to clean their feathers carefully.

When it is dark, kori bustards lay down for the night.

Most kori bustards sleep alone, but chicks sleep next to their mothers.

Kori Bustard Body Map

beak

crest

back

neck

leg

Glossary

crest feathers that stick up on some birds' heads

female animal that can become a mother when it is grown up

grassland land where mostly grasses grow

hyena wild animal that mostly lives in grasslands in Africa. It looks like a dog.

insect small animal with six legs. Ants, beetles, and bees are insects.

jackal wild animal that lives in Africa and Asia. It looks like a dog or a fox.

male animal that can become a father when it is grown up

Find Out More

Books

Burnie, David. *Bird (DK Eyewitness Books)*. New York: DK Children, 2008.

Gray, Samantha, and Sarah Walker. *Birds (Eye Wonder)*. New York: DK Children, 2002.

Websites

http://koribustardssp.org/Home_Page.php

http://www.arkive.org/kori-bustard/ardeotis-kori/info.html

Index